GU01018662

The Essential

Gambler

The Essential

Gambler

Edited by
GRAHAM SHARPE

ROBERT HALE • LONDON

© *Graham Sharpe 1995*
First published in Great Britain 1995

ISBN 0 7090 5510 2

Robert Hale Limited
Clerkenwell House
Clerkenwell Green
London EC1R 0HT

2 4 6 8 10 9 7 5 3 1

Printed and bound in Hong Kong by
Bookbuilders Limited

Preface

For all its faults, the National Lottery has had at least one positive long-term result — it has made gambling respectable and acceptable to the public at large. A few will still carp, but they are now in a vociferous but statistically insignificant minority.

The hype, razamatazz and glamorous promotions surrounding the Lottery have swept away all but the most firmly established and deeply felt objections to gambling in general. And not before time.

More hypocritical and self-righteous nonsense has been spouted by those who would deny us the right to gamble than on virtually any other subject – including alcohol, tobacco and sex! A sickening moral superiority and loathsomely patronizing attitude has always permeated the rhetoric of those who would save us from ourselves and keep us from our flutters, wagers, bets and punts.

Much of the material you will read in this book is anti-gambling. Read it and marvel at the breathtaking cant and humbug rolled out in increasingly desperate efforts to protect us from our own failings. But applaud and congratulate those with the foresight and strength of character to speak up on behalf of the gambler.

You will gather from my remarks that I fall into the pro-gambling camp, as you might expect from someone who earns his living from the profits of bookmaking, as Media Relations Manager of William Hill. Nevertheless, I have thoroughly enjoyed wallowing in the deep and wide waters of the anti-gambling ocean of literature in order to emerge not drowning but waving and clutching much material from such sources to illustrate the breadth of feeling engendered by the subject. I have also compiled a goodly selection of pithy and worthwhile remarks from pro-gambling sources to even up the balance.

I believe you will find clear winners, and gallant losers along with the also-rans in this varied and diverse collection of gambling quotations. I trust that it is a dead cert that you will discover more in the way of hot favourites than cold comfort from the pages of the book.

GRAHAM SHARPE

Acknowledgements

Thanks are due to the following for permission to include copyright material: Cambridge University Press for extracts from *Gambling and Speculation* by Reuven Brenner with Gabrielle A. Brenner (1990); David Spanier for extracts from his column in the *Independent*; the *Guardian* for a number of extracts; Michael Harris, chief executive of the *Racing Post* for extracts from that newspaper; Tom Clarke, editor of the *Sporting Life* for extracts from that newspaper; Sir Clement Freud for extracts from his writings on the subject of gambling; Garth Burden, deputy managing editor for extracts from the *Daily*

Mail; Geraldine Ranson, press officer for The Methodist Church for extracts from a press release from that body; Diana Pepper, Syndication Manager for material from the *Independent*; Ron Pollard, former director of Ladbrokes, for a quote and for another, unsolicited, which he attributed to the late William Hill; Robert Hardman; Lord Oaksey; Martin Vander Weyer for an extract from the *Daily Telegraph*; Simon Barnes for an extract from his column in *The Times*; and Constable & Co. Ltd for an extract from a Damon Runyan story.

Every effort has been made to seek permission for copyright material. Apologies are offered to those I may have overlooked or whom I was unable to trace.

Gambling consists of an agreement between parties with respect to an unascertained outcome that, depending on the outcome, there will be a redistribution of advantage (usually but not always monetary) among those parties.

ROYAL COMMISSION ON GAMBLING
July 1978

Gaming is the mother of lies and perjuries.

JOHN OF SALISBURY
BISHOP OF CHARTRES (1175)

It [gambling] is the child of avarice, the brother of iniquity and the father of mischief.

GEORGE WASHINGTON
15 January 1783
and he was a racehorse owner!

There are two times in a man's life when he should not speculate: When he can't afford it and when he can.

MARK TWAIN
Puddenhead Wilson's New Calendar
(1835-1910)

Gaming is a principle inherent in human nature.

EDMUND BURKE
11 February 1780
in the House of Commons

The roulette table pays nobody except him that keeps it. Nevertheless, a passion for gambling is common though a passion for keeping roulette tables is unknown.

GEORGE BERNARD SHAW (1856-1950)

The best throw of the dice is to throw them away.

SCOTTISH PROVERB

A wager is a fool's argument.

ENGLISH SAYING

In betting on races, there are two elements that are never lacking: hope as hope, and an incomplete recollection of the past.

E. V. LUCAS
New York Times
7 October 1951

The people who think they can wind up ahead of the races are everybody who has ever won a bet.

OGDEN NASH
Pocket Book (1902-71)

It is death which gives gambling and hedonism their true meaning.

ALBERT CAMUS
Notebooks, 1935-42

There is enough energy wasted in poker to make a hundred thousand successful men every year.

ARTHUR BRISBANE
The Book of Today

Gaming is an enchanting witchery, gotten betwixt idleness and avarice; An itching disease, that makes some scratch the head, whilst others, as if they were bitten by a Tarantula, are laughing themselves to death: Or lastly, it is a paralytical distemper, which seizing the arm the man cannot choose but shake his elbow. It hath this ill property above all other vices, that it renders a man incapable of prosecuting any serious action and makes him always unsatisfied with his own condition. He is either lifted up to the top of mad joy with success, or plunged to the bottom of despair by misfortune.

CHARLES COTTON
The Compleat Gamester
1674

Betting clerks, and betting servants of all grades, once detected after a grave warning, should be firmly dismissed.

CHARLES DICKENS
Household Words
26 June 1852

With the large majority of those who habitually bet, sheer greed is the incentive. They are lazy and have little or no interest in work. They seek a straight and easy way to wealth. They hear of large sums won on races and they wish to share in this delightfully simple method of acquiring wealth. If men were neither lazy nor greedy, if they found sufficient stimulus and reward in forwarding the work of the world there would be no betting.

PROFESSOR MARCUS DODS
On Betting
1897

There can be no whole-hearted love of sport where there is betting. To a man who habitually bets, there is no attraction in a game of whist or billiards, or in a horse race, on which no money depends. Sport in itself ceases to be of interest to the man who has staked a large amount upon the issue.

PROFESSOR MARCUS DODS
On Betting
1897

There are some thousands of bookmakers in our own country. Out of whose pockets do they pick so comfortable a living? Out of the pocket of their dupes who so bountifully contribute to the maintenance of their worst enemies.

PROFESSOR MARCUS DODS
On Betting
1897

Betting is a prolific source of crime. As betting is largely indulged in by boys whose wages amount to seven or eight shillings a week, and by clerks who have less than a hundred a year, it is obvious that losses must strongly tempt them to embezzlement and theft.

PROFESSOR MARCUS DODS
On Betting
1897

There is no one good thing which can be pointed to as produced by betting. It is the prolific mother of a brood without exception evil.

PROFESSOR MARCUS DODS
On Betting
1897

I have lost enough money to build a casino.
SAMUEL LEWIS
Rueful nineteenth-century gambler

The most sensible advice that may be given to
would-be gamblers, or inventors of systems to
be used at Monte Carlo, may be summed up in
a single word: 'Don't'.
FRANÇOIS BLANC (b.1806)
the nineteenth-century entrepreneur who
established the *Monte Carlo Casino*

17

A gambler with a System must be, to a greater or lesser extent, insane.

GEORGE AUGUSTUS SALA (1828-95)
English writer and journalist

The Kursaal is a public set of rooms, finer than some palaces, all supported by gambling. Herein I beheld such a set of damnable faces – French, Italian, and Russian, with dull English in quantities – as were never seen out of Hell before!

THOMAS CARLYLE
impression of an 1852 trip to the gaming rooms of Homburg

If I play with sharpers and win, I am sure to be paid, but if I win of gentlemen, they frequently behave so genteelly that I get nothing but words and polite apologies for my money.

THE EARL OF CHESTERFIELD
An eighteenth-century gambler explains his predilection for playing with dubious characters.

He would be in prison if his creditors did not occasionally release him to play and cheat my Lord Chesterfield, as the only chance they have for recovering their money.

HORACE WALPOLE

1755

casting doubt on the wisdom of this policy by his comment on a Moravian Baron at Bath.

We have often wondered that the physicians of the place prescribe gaming to their patients, in order to keep their minds free from business and thought, that the water on an undisturbed mind may have the greater effect, when indeed one cross throw at play must sour a man's blood more than ten glasses of water will sweeten it, especially for such great sums as they throw for every day at Bath.

DANIEL DEFOE

1772

following a trip to the waters and gaming rooms of Bath.

The Church and Rooms the other day
Opened their books for prayer and play
The church got six: Hoyle sixty seven.
How great the odds of Hell to Heaven.

ANONYMOUS EARLY EIGHTEENTH-CENTURY
POEM
published after Bath Abbey and Bath's
Lower Rooms gambling den both
launched an appeal for funds on the same
day

The gambler is apparently the last optimist;
he is a creature totally unmoved by experience. His belief in ultimate success cannot be
shattered by financial loss, however great. He
did not win today? So what? Tomorrow will
be lucky. He's lost again? It doesn't prove a
thing; someday he's bound to win.

E. BERGLER
Psychology of Gambling
1957

Most people think that poker is a game. It isn't, man. It's work. You have to work at it like anything else and you get payoffs. You can't just sit down and play. I go and think about the players and the game for a while and draw up a game plan. I don't like to play long hours because I'm concentrating and figuring odds all the time. Hell, I work less hours a month than a doctor and I can take vacations any time I want to. This is what I want to do. This is my career.

> ANONYMOUS POKER PLAYER TO WRITER
> D.M. HAYANO
> 1977

Who is the most important person in the racing industry? The breeder? The owner? The trainer? The administrator? The bookie? The jockey or stablehand? No, it is none of these. The most important person is the mug punter.

> J. WILLIAMS
> 1990
> Australian writer

Compulsive gambling is an illness, progressive in its nature, which cannot be cured but can be arrested.

> GAMBLERS ANONYMOUS
> 1977

Gambling is the sure way of getting nothing for something.

    WILSON MIZNER (1876-1933)
    American writer

Gambling may be wicked; it is certainly very stupid; but it happens to be an innate characteristic of mankind, and that is really all one need say about it.

    GENERAL PIERRE POLOVTSOFF
    President of the International Sporting Club in his history, *Monte Carlo Casino* 1937

England Expects Every Man To Do His Duty . . . much less should he refuse to profit by the golden chance of enriching himself for life, which the State Lottery now offers to all adventurers.

    Government poster on behalf of the Lottery
    January 1810

I've been a gambler all my life. It separates the winners from the losers, and that's the excitement. Like you can go out to Las Vegas in a $45,000 Cadillac and go home in a $7500

bus that isn't yours! That's how dangerous
the table is.

RYAN O'NEAL
actor
1985

Satan seeketh to sow dissension and hatred
among you by means of wine and lots.

THE KORAN
Chapter V

The gambler masochistically enjoys his fear of
losing and continues it as long as possible,
because when he leaves the table or race-
course to take up his ordinary life some really
intolerable fear awaits him; the smaller fear
of losing his money is by comparison a pleasure.

RALPH GREENSON
US psychologist

The fluttering movements of a card dealer's
hands, the thrust and withdrawal movements
of the croupier's rake, and the shaking of the
dice box can all be identified with sublima-
tions of copulation or masturbation.

SIGMUND FREUD (1856-1939)

Gambling is a way of buying hope on credit.

ALAN WYKES
Gambling
1964

Don't be a gambler; once a gambler, always a gambler.

JOHN W. GATES
1909
warning from the 54-year-old 'Bet-a-million' Gates, legendary US gambler, to a Church conference in Texas

I am not the least interested in the game, nor in whether I win or lose. I am only interested in whether or not the amount is large enough to be noticed.

ANDRE CITROEN (*d.* 1935)
French motor-car tycoon

I agree that gambling is anti-social, but at least it keeps people away from television.

ANONYMOUS US CLERGYMAN TO AUTHOR
BERNARD NEWMAN,
reported in his 1960s book, *Mr Kennedy's America*

Even if gambling were altogether an evil, still, on account of the very large number of people who play, it would seem to be a natural evil. For that very reason it ought to be discussed by a medieval doctor like one of the incurable diseases; for in every evil there is at least evil, in every infamy at least infamy, and similarly in loss of time and fortune. Also, it has been the custom of philosophers to deal with the vices in order that advantage might be drawn from them, as for example in the case of anger. Thus it is not absurd for me to discuss gambling, not in order to praise it but in order to point out the advantages in it, and, of course, also its disadvantages, in order that they may be reduced to a minimum.

GIROLAMO CARDANO (1501-76)
Italian Renaissance physician and mathematician, the first to relate mathematics to gambling in his *Book of Games and Chance*

A gentleman is a man who will pay his gambling debts even when he knows he has been cheated.

COUNT LEO TOLSTOY (1828-1910)

You don't gamble to win. You gamble so you can gamble the next day.
BERT AMBROSE
Band leader

If I were you, I would not bet. But if you must bet – BET!
WILLIAM I'ANSON (*d.* 1881)
Advice to his eldest son from racehorse trainer
Biographical Encyclopaedia of British Flat Racing, 1978

It [gambling] can become wrong when it is inconsistent with our duties or when it is carried to excess.
CARDINAL HUME
14 July 1977

For most men (till by losing render'd sager)
Will back their own opinions with a wager.
  BYRON (1788-1824)
  Beppo

It is a fine thing to get a peck or a bushel of
gold just by betting for it, the tremulous rap-
ture of mingled hope and fear is almost com-
pensation enough even if one loses. Next to
the pleasure of winning is the pleasure of losing; only stagnation is unendurable.
  HUBERT HOWE BANCROFT
  California Inter Pocula
  1888
  US historian

At a meeting of the citizens of Vicksburg on
Saturday the 4th of July [1835], it was
Resolved, That a notice be given to all professional GAMBLERS, that the citizens of
Vicksburg are resolved to exclude them from
this place and its vicinity, and that twenty-
four hours notice be given them to leave the
place.
      the people of the Mississippi town meant
      what they said – they later lynched five
      gamblers who didn't shift quickly enough.
      Mississippi Department of Archives and
      History

27

Few men are going to be deterred by the scientific assurance that all can not be successful in a lottery. It would not be a very attractive lottery if they could.

A. P. HERBERT
Pools Pilot
1953

The big difference between Lotto [a US lottery] and life is that in this game everyone has the same chance.

GERALD WILLIAMS
Newsweek
2 September 1985
Harlem resident

Resolutely Enforce the Central Committee's Strict Injunction against Gambling.

THE TIMES
17 August 1994
large sign stretched above the finishing post besides the odds board at the Peking Country Horse Racing Club, China.

We detest begging, we spend large sums in the anti-gambling movement, but we publish betting tips because we cannot sell our newspapers without them.

LORD SANDS

1918

the most delicate of hypocrisies from this newspaper proprietor

Betting and gambling of every kind, is in itself wrong and immoral. I do not say that every man who bets is an immoral man. Far from it: many really honest men bet; but that is because they have not considered what they are doing. Betting is wrong: because it is wrong to take your neighbour's money without giving him anything in return. Earn from him what you will, and as much as you can. All labour, even the lowest drudgery is honourable; but betting is not labouring nor earning; it is getting money without earning it, and more, it is getting money, or trying to get it, out of your neighbour's ignorance.

CHARLES KINGSLEY (1819-75)
On Betting and Gambling

Money won by gambling . . . is not won without self-seeking and love of self, and not without sin.

MARTIN LUTHER (1483-1546)

If you're on your tod and earning money, you can bet what you like. But if you're betting money which should be used to buy food or pay the rent, then that's wrong . . . I never like to bet with friends. I like to lose and win from a company which is faceless. Like a casino – they're the enemy.

OMAR SHARIF
quoted by Nick Reeves, *Sporting Life*, 22 August 1994

A ruler should encourage gambling among his enemies, and put it down by military force at home.

NICCOLO MACHIAVELLI (1469-1527)

Gaming is become so much the Fashion among the Beau-Monde, that he who in company should appear ignorant of the Games in Vogue, would be reckoned low-bred and hardly fit for Conversation.

RICHARD SEYMOUR
The Court Gamester
1722

People who thought it was evil are playing slot machines and lightning does not strike them.

BILL THOMPSON Professor of Public Administration at the University of Nevada
on the increasing number of Las Vegas gamblers

British hypocrisy knows few bounds. Fruit machines are banned in betting shops, a controlled environment, but are freely available elsewhere to kids. We are totally mad.

JIM CREMIN
Racing Post
19 August 1994

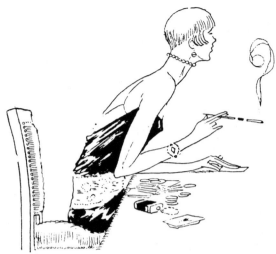

To permit the bookmaker to enter the athletic ground, and ply his calling therein, is to write the doom of legitimate sport, for rascality follows in the wake of the betting man, and legitimate rivalry will be at an end.

THE BISHOP OF CHESTER

addressing the Chester Gymnastic Club, April 1889

Most people bet with their heads, not over them, and realize that gambling and speculation are good servants and bad masters.

REUVEN AND GABRIELLE A. BRENNER

Gambling and Speculation

1990

Since the World is but a kind of Lottery, why should Gamesters be begrudged the drawing of a Prize? If . . . a Man has his Estate by Chance, why should not my chance take it away from him?

> JEREMY COLLIER
> *An Essay Upon Gaming*
> 1713

There can be no question but that the effects of gambling are all evil, unmitigated by any redeeming qualities.

> MAJOR SETON CHURCHILL
> *Betting and Gambling*
> 1894

In gambling it would seem impossible that through the dark cloud of moral pollution which is hovering over the country, a single gleam of sunlight should shine.

> MAJOR SETON CHURCHILL
> *Betting and Gambling*
> 1894

It is, of course, possible for a gambler to believe in God, and even to pray to God that he may have success in his gambling, but such prayers must be an abomination to the Lord, for it is assumed by those who offer them that God can bless the pursuits of iniquity.

> MAJOR SETON CHURCHILL
> *Betting and Gambling*
> 1894

Plenty of men who are now gamblers were originally good fellows.

> MAJOR SETON CHURCHILL
> *Betting and Gambling*
> 1894

True sport and manliness are being seriously damaged by this spirit of gambling . . . In the days of the Romans the principal reason why the authorities endeavoured to stop games in which pecuniary gain was at stake, was that they were found to have a distinct tendency to make young men effeminate and unmanly . . . In our own country, too, the ground on which gambling was first prohibited was not its demoralizing effect, but its effeminate influence on young men.

> MAJOR SETON CHURCHILL
> *Betting and Gambling*
> 1894

If all men were to turn gamblers for a living, they would become like wolves searching the wastes of the earth without a living being to prey on, and forced to turn cannibals, or be honest, or die.

> MAJOR SETON CHURCHILL
> reporting a Dr Lambert in
> *Betting and Gambling*
> 1894

The sudden loss, or the equally sudden gain, of gambling has a most injurious effect on the working man, producing an amount of excitement incompatible with steady painstaking labour.

> MAJOR SETON CHURCHILL
> *Betting and Gambling*
> 1894

It is because gambling, when it takes a firm hold, demoralises a man, because it brutalises and materialises his nature, because it either absorbs his spirit with the lust of greed, or enervates him by excitement without enthusiasm, that gambling is wrong.

> *The Spectator*
> 1894

When you've risked about ten times more than you can afford and savoured the flow of adrenalin, it is hard to get excited about anything else.

JEFFREY BERNARD
reported in the *Racing Post*
12 August 1994

Every bet represents an artificially induced crisis. Life squeezed down to a moment of all or nothing. You oscillate from feelings of wild abandonment to icy fear and back again within an instant.

MARK COTON
One Hundred Hints for Better Betting
1994

We're encouraged to believe that it's okay for the Lottery to rob us blind because so much of the money is going to good causes.

DEREK MCGOVERN
Racing Post
19 November 1994

Win or lose, betting fulfils recreational needs; it provides entertainment, excitement, sense of involvement in live sport, relief from boredom or worry, and in the case of big accumulative bets the hope of deliverance from the daily round. Losses can be regarded (albeit not necessarily consciously) as a form of payment for the enjoyment obtained from the betting experience.

> DAVID BENNETT
> *Sporting Life*
> 13 August 1994

Gambling is neither an immoral nor a noble exercise; it is motivated by both foolish and rational considerations.

> ALEX RUBNER
> author of *Fringe Benefits: The Golden Chains* (1962) and *The Economics of Gambling* (1966)

I believe in pushing my luck. But not in giving it an almighty shove.

> LORD BERNARD DELFONT
> *Daily Mail*, 29 July 1994
> reported shortly after his death
> after quitting whilst ahead at a Cannes casino

To anti gambling devotees, private, uncontrolled gambling, and better still illegal ventures conducted under the veil of secrecy by crooks, are an obvious ideal, because the public is fleeced and this may cure some of them of their sordid habits.

ALEX RUBNER
The Economics of Gambling (1966)

Gaming corrupts our dispositions, and teaches us a habit of hostility against all mankind.

THOMAS JEFFERSON
1787
US President

Lottery, which like love is the game of chance par excellence, takes advantage of the beauty that we can admire in the dreamy eyes of so many lovely Spanish women.

V. MOLITOR
a bizarre comment by the director of the Luxembourg National Lottery, in 1963

If successful gamblers die broke it is probably because nothing can take the place of the risk. The cosy assumption that gamblers are subconsciously trying to lose has always seemed the purest nonsense to me.

IAN CARNABY
Sporting Life
21 July 1994

Greed is the punter's greatest downfall. You can eat only one dinner, why attempt to go for more?

JACK HOLT
Sporting Life
29 July 1994
racehorse trainer

I would argue that putting money on horses is better for children than eating sweets; both are addictive but £1 each way on the Tote neither causes cavities nor induces obesity. On the whole betting children are lean and healthy children.

SIR CLEMENT FREUD
Sporting Life
2 August 1994

If I suddenly had a large increase in income, I have no doubt that I should spend a large part of it on smoking, eating, drinking, gambling and similar deplorable recreations; and I decline to debase myself morally on that account.

> ANTHONY CROSLAND
> *The Listener*
> 8 December 1955

Legislation needed to be brought up to date, given that King George III was on the Throne and Lord North was Prime Minister when the Sunday Observance Act 1780 was passed.

> MICHAEL FORSYTH
> on the introduction of Sunday betting which became legal from January 1995

Of all kill-time occupations, gambling seems to exercise the strongest spell. Hence the devotion to Monte Carlo of generations of people who had so much time on their hands that they were ready to spend any amount of money in order to kill it.

> *NEW STATESMAN AND NATION*
> 28 July 1934

No one on this earth knows whether gambling is seen in the celestial terrain as an unforgivable sin.

ALEX RUBNER
The Economics of Gambling
1966

The evidence we have found has led us to the conclusion that the negative image of gamblers, of speculators and of gambling is due to prejudice, to the distorted image heavily promoted by some powerful groups who, however, have not had much evidence to support their views.

REUVEN AND GABRIELLE A. BRENNER
preface to *Gaming and Speculation*
1990

Gamblers are neither mentally ill nor criminals . . . gambling does not lead its practitioners to poverty. It is, rather, the other way around. Some of the poor and the frustrated gamble. Gambling is for them a channel of hope, not a disease.

JACKET 'BLURB'
Gambling and Speculation by Reuven and Gabrielle A. Brenner
1990

When I was young, people called me a gambler. As the scale of my operations increased I became known as a speculator. Now I am called a banker. But I have been doing the same thing all the time.

SIR ERNEST CASSEL
Private banker to King Edward VII

You can't really call someone you're trying to carve up for hundreds of pounds your close friend. But I have mates now among the guys I play against every day. It's a strange kind of relationship, really. Maybe we're all poker addicts, but there's a kind of brotherly feeling. We try to f*** each other, but we don't take it personally.

Is poker better than sex? You may think

that's a daft question, but its something I've thought about a lot. How long does a f*** last? A poker game can go on for 12 hours. When you're on a winning streak, the feeling is better than any other feeling I know. It's aggression and money, you know? Sex doesn't come into it.

COLIN HAYES,
Evening Standard magazine
15 July 1994
thoughts of would-be professional poker player

The advent of a National Lottery in Britain, however, gives the state a direct stake in gambling. Down the ages church and state have always been opposed to gambling. Now, for the first time (no matter how the ministers may protest), the government will be encouraging people to gamble. Gambling used to be condemned as a sin. Then it became tolerated as a sort of social offence (like prostitution). Nowadays it is seen, all round the world, as part of the entertainment business. If people want to gamble they should be allowed to do so. Setting the limits is the trick.

DAVID SPANIER
The Independent
13 July 1994

Casinos in Britain remain a secret society . . . For in gambling, the besetting English sin is hypocrisy. Nowhere is the pretence that gambling is not really part of our culture more suspect than in casino regulation. Its motivating spirit stems far more from mandarin ideas of protecting people from themselves than from popular taste.

Thus, in Britain's casinos there is no entertainment, no music, no slot machines (apart from two per casino), no drinks at the table, restricted hours of play and, above all, the absurd rule that you must sign on 48 hours in advance if you want to play, in case (perish the thought) someone might walk into a casino off the street just on impulse.

DAVID SPANIER
The Independent
13 July 1994

Most gamesters begin at small game; and, by degrees, if their money, or estates, hold out, they rise to great sums; some have played, first of all, their money, then their rings, coach and horses, even their wearing clothes and perukes; and then, such a farm; and, at last, perhaps a lordship.

ANONYMOUS
The Nicker Nicked; or the Cheats of Gaming Discovered
1669

If a man has a competent estate of his own, and plays whether himself or another man shall have it, it is extreme folly; if his estate be small, then to hazard the loss even of that and reduce himself to absolute beggary is direct madness. Besides, it has been generally observed, that the loss of one hundred pounds shall do you more prejudice in disquieting your mind than the gain of two hundred pounds shall do you good, were you sure to keep it.

ANONYMOUS
The Nicker Nicked; or the cheats of Gaming Discovered
1669

The law should take no cognisance whatever of wagers.

ADVICE FROM THE 1844 SELECT COMMITTEE APPOINTED TO REPORT TO THE HOUSE OF LORDS

If private individuals choose to make wagers with each other there seems to be no good reason why they should be prevented from doing so, or why they should be punished for so doing; but neither on the other hand does there seem to be any sufficient reason why the valuable time of the Courts of law should be consumed by adjudicating disputes which may arise between individuals in consequence of such wagers.

1844 SELECT COMMITTEE REPORT TO HOUSE OF COMMONS

If you wanna make money in a casino, own one.

STEVE WYNN
Vegas Casino owner
quoted by David Spanier in *All Right, Okay, You Win* (1992)

A man dropped down at the door of White's; he was carried into the Club . Was he dead or not? The odds were immediately given and taken for and against. It was proposed to bleed him. Those who had taken odds that the man was dead protested that the use of the lancet would affect the fairness of the bet; he was therefore left to himself and presently died – to the great satisfaction of those who had bet for that event.

HORACE WALPOLE (1717-97)

If any person by fraud in playing at, or betting upon, games, should win any money or valuable thing, he should forfeit five times the sum so won, be deemed infamous, and be whipped as a perjurer.

DETAIL FROM AN ACT OF 1710
not repealed until 1845

Every person playing or betting by way of wagering in any street, road, highway or other open and public place, or in any open place to which the public have or are permitted to have access, at or with any table or instrument of gaming, or any coin, card, token or other article used as an instrument or means of such wagering or gaming, at any game or pretended game of chance, shall be deemed a rogue and vagabond.

DETAIL FROM AN ACT OF 1873

Casinos don't mind giving away afternoon teas. They know that on 95 per cent of cases gastro-generosity leads to consumer-guilt manifested by a visit to the tables.

SIR CLEMENT FREUD

48

I remember an occasion when Robert Morley and I had dinner and he announced over the smoked salmon that we would not be going on to a casino. He explained that the previous weekend he had written to all the casinos of which he was a member to announce his resignation and request he be barred if brought in as someone else's guest.

SIR CLEMENT FREUD

According to my view, a wagering contract is one by which two persons, professing to hold opposite views touching the issue of a future uncertain event, mutually agree that, dependent upon the determination of that event, one shall win from the other, and that other shall pay or hand over to him, a sum of money or other stake; neither of the contracting parties having any other interests in that contract than the sum or stake he will so win or lose, there being no other real consideration for the making of such contract by either of the parties. It is essential to a wagering contract that each party may under it either win or lose, whether he will win or lose being dependent on the issue of the event, and, therefore, remaining uncertain until that issue is known. If either of the parties may win but cannot lose, or may lose but cannot win, it is not a wagering contract.

DEFINITIVE EXPLANATION OF THE TERM 'BET' coined in 1892 by Judge, Mr Justice Hawkins and used and referred to for many years after.

Next to that of luxury, naturally follows the offence of gaming, which is generally introduced to supply or retrieve the expenses occasioned by the former . . . . But, taken in any light, it is an offence of the most alarming nature, tending by necessary consequences to promote public theft, idleness and debauchery among those of a lower class; and among persons of superior rank, it hath frequently been attended with the sudden ruin and desolation of ancient and opulent families, an abandoned prostitution of every principle of honour and virtue, and too often hath ended in self-murder.

MR BLACKSTONE
Commentaries, IV, 1765
Member of Parliament and lawyer

We cannot put a stop to gambling by legislation. Efforts have been made in that direction before now and no one has found how to suppress an insuppressible instinct in the human race.

PRIME MINISTER STANLEY BALDWIN
House of Commons
11 June 1936

Man is not a born gambler but, from his experiences in life, he acquires a fascination for the elements of chance, and seeking to emulate his elders, he attempts to exploit these factors in pursuance of reward. It would appear that gambling in the betting sense is a thread in the pattern of social evolution – a thread that has remained unbroken since the dawn of time.

J. PHILIP JONES
Gambling Yesterday and Today
1973

Nearly every gambler flatters himself that with just one more shot his luck will turn, and he will reap a rich harvest. Because of this delusion the Casino always wins in the end.

GENERAL PIERRE POLOVTSOFF
Monte Carlo Casino
1937

I do not believe in systems. There is only one thing that will enable you to win at Monte Carlo or anywhere else and that is luck. If you experience a run of bad luck, then stop playing. If you win, then be firm with yourself, pocket your money and go out into the fresh air.

GENERAL PIERRE POLOVTSOFF
Monte Carlo Casino
1937

If the description of this event in the Book of Revelation is anything to go by, I doubt if the bookies will be open that day for you to collect your winnings.

REPLY FROM LAMBETH PALACE TO GAMBLER C. PEPLER OF CHATHAM IN KENT
who had staked a bet with William Hill that the Archbishop of Canterbury would confirm the Second Coming and wrote to the Head of the Church of England seeking confirmation that the event had already occurred
1993

The next best thing to gambling and winning is gambling and losing.

NICK 'THE GREEK' DANDALOS
Professional gambler
died penniless, Christmas Day, 1966

Gambling is an escape from the routine and boredom characteristic of much of modern industrial life in which the sense of creation and the instinct of workmanship have been lost.

H. A. BLOCH
American Journal of Sociology
November 1951

I invest, you bet, he gambles.
TRADITIONAL MOTTO

Professional gambling today is the most lucrative, most destructive and withal most widely tolerated form of crime in this country. Each year the revenues that pass into the coffers of 'Gambling Inc' are used to bribe elected officials, to oil political machines and to corrupt police and other law-enforcement agencies on a scale so staggering it has not yet been truly measured.

THE NATION (New York)
22 October 1960

Gambling is on the increase. It has become a national vice. There is no doubt that all the legalising of betting shops and of other forms of gambling has encouraged the gambling habit. Gambling is closely linked with the widespread desire for money. Love of money, St Paul said, is the root of all evil.

Sunday School Chronicle
25 April 1963

The essence of gambling consists in an abandonment of reason, and inhibition of the factors of human control. A practice so corrupting to the intelligence not only of the

habitue, but even of the casual spectator, stands condemned as a formidable enemy of education and of intellectual order.
JOHN A HOBSON
Philosopher
1905

Gambling is merely a method whereby wealth is redistributed from the possession of the many into the hands of the few.
VIRGIL W. PETERSON
Director of the Chicago Crime
Commission
1951

Judaism regards gambling on the same level as sex or alcohol; a pleasurable activity if done in appropriate circumstances but harmful if it is taken beyond certain bounds.
THE JEWISH INFORMATION & MEDIA SERVICE
Press Release from the Reform
Synagogues of Great Britain
9 November 1994

This country has become a gamblers' paradise, more wide-open in this respect than any other comparable country.

ROY JENKINS, HOME SECRETARY (1966)

The spread of the gambling habit is one of the most disquieting events of the time for those particularly who believe in self-government and in an intelligent democracy using its political powers to secure moral and social ends.

RAMSAY MACDONALD (1866-1937)
first British Labour Prime Minister

Gambling challenges the view of life which the Christian Church exists to uphold and extend. Its glorification of mere chance is a denial of the Divine Order in nature. To risk money haphazardly is to disregard the insistence of the Church of every age of living faith that possessions are a trust, and that men must account to God for their use. The persistent appeal to covetousness is fundamentally opposed to the unselfishness which was taught by Jesus Christ and by the New Testament as a whole. The attempt (which is inseparable from gambling) to make out of the inevitable loss and possible suffering of others is the antithesis of that love of one's neighbour on which the Lord insisted.

WILLIAM TEMPLE
Archbishop of York
To the 1932 Royal Commission on Lotteries and Betting

A vast engine of demoralisation.
BENJAMIN DISRAELI (1804-81)
on gambling

There is no such thing as luck. It is all mathematics. There are three kinds of cards — good cards, bad cards and indifferent cards. You must play them according to what they are. That is not a contradiction. You may have luck for an hour or two, even a day or two, even a week. But what people call luck is merely an established fact seen through the spectacles of after events.

NICO ZOGRAPHOS (*d*. 1953)
renowned 1920s and 30s baccarat gambler, head of Greek syndicate which operated a famous no-limit game

As they increased it was found that their continuance corrupted the morals, and encouraged a spirit of Speculation and Gambling among the lower classes of the people; thousands of whom fell victims to their insinuating and tempting allurements.

FROM AN ANONYMOUS EPITAPH TO THE MEMORY OF THE STATE LOTTERY
published in 1826 to mark the drawing of the last Government-run Lottery

By the establishment of State lotteries, a spirit of gambling, injurious in the highest degree, to the morals of the people, is encouraged and provoked.

MR LYTTLETON, MP
moving for the banning of Lotteries, 1819

That curse of the England of our time, betting upon horse racing, which can be compared to nothing but a social cancer, eating into the very vitals of the nation; and it is especially a pity that so noble an animal as the horse should be made the unconscious medium of such a degrading passion as gambling.

JOHN ASHTON
The History of Gambling in England
1899

Gaming was now managed in such a manner, as rendered skill and dexterity of no advantage; for the spirit of play having over-spread the land, like a pestilence, raged to such a degree of madness and desperation, that the unhappy people who were infected, laid aside all thoughts of amusement, economy, or caution, and risqued their fortunes upon issues equally extravagant, childish and absurd.

TOBIAS SMOLLETT
Adventures of Ferdinand Fathom (c.1750)

In Vegas everything is done to make you gamble and forget all else. There is food and drink and music and women – who all play their part in eliminating methodist principles from your mind.

SIR CLEMENT FREUD
Sporting Life
1 March 1994

The betting laws of this country are in a tremendous mess, and something ought to be done about it; but nothing is done. Nothing will be done. It is a hopeless mess, and everybody is afraid to touch it.

MR JUSTICE SWIFT
Yorkshire Evening Post
18 May 1936

There is nothing that wears out a fine Face like the vigils of the Card Table, and those cutting Passions which naturally attend them. Hollow Eyes, haggard Looks, and pale Complexions, are the natural Indications of a Female Gamester. Her Morning Sleeps are not able to repair her Midnight Watchings.

FROM A STUDY OF FEMALE GAMBLING
The Guardian
29 July 1713

All Play Debts must be paid in Specie, or by an Equivalent. The Man who plays beyond his Income, pawns his Estate; the woman must find out something else to Mortgage when her Pin Money is gone. The Husband has his Lands to dispose of, the Wife, her Person.

FROM A STUDY OF FEMALE GAMBLING
The Guardian
29 July 1713

5 April 1805. The sum lately lost at play by a lady of high rank is variously stated. Some say it does not amount to more than £200,000, while others assert that it is little short of £700,000. Her Lord is very unhappy on the occasion, and is still undecided with respect to the best mode to be adopted in the unfortunate predicament.

MORNING POST

It is lamentable to see a lovely woman destroying her health and beauty at six o'clock in the morning at a gaming-table. Can any woman expect to give her husband a vigorous and healthy offspring, whose mind, night after night, is thus distracted, and whose body is relaxed by anxiety and the fatigue of late hours? It is impossible.

COLONEL GEORGE HANGER, FOURTH LORD COLERAINE
Life, Adventures and Opinions of Colonel George Hanger
1801

The greatest advantage in gambling lies in not playing at all.

GIROLAMO CARDANO (1501-76)
Book on Games of Chance

At some of our first Boarding Schools, the fair pupils are now taught to play whist and casino. It is calculated that a clever child, by its Cards, may pay for its own education.

THE TIMES
2 November 1797

So completely has gambling got the better of dancing, that at a private Ball, last week, a gentleman asking a young lady, from Bath, to dance the next two dances, she very ingenuously replied, 'Yes, if you will play two rubbers at Casino'.

THE TIMES
22 December 1797

In some places they call Gaming Houses 'Academies'; but I know not why they should inherit that honourable name, since there is nothing to be learn'd there, unless it be Sleight of Hand, which is sometimes at the Expence of all our Money, to get that of other Men's by Fraud and Cunning.

THOMAS BROWN (1663-1704)
The Works of Thomas Brown

A man who can play delightfully on a guitar and keep a knife in his boot would make an excellent poker player.

W. J. FLORENCE
Handbook on Poker
1891

As for national lotteries, the real money always ends up subsidising government expenditure and it must make politicians roar with laughter to see citizens eagerly queuing to pay taxes, under the mistaken impression that they're having a flutter.

VICTOR LEWIS-SMITH
Evening Standard
16 November 1994

Bingo kills the mind.
DR WARNER SCHAIE
Pennsylvania State University
February 1994

It doesn't matter who wins or loses, only who
ends up with the money.
LAWRENCE REVERE
Mid-twentieth century blackjack gambler,
who died in 1977 a millionaire

Britain's puritanical hotchpotch of betting
regulations is a relic of the conviction that all
gambling, though not an actual deadly sin, is
the sort of improper behaviour which, like
buying dirty books, ought to be discouraged.
LORD OAKSEY

Gambling is the great leveller. All men are
equal – at cards.
NIKOLAI GOGOL
The Gamblers
1842

True luck consists not in holding the best of the cards at the table; Luckiest he who knows just when to rise and go home.

JOHN HAY
Distichs
1871

Adventure upon all the tickets in the lottery and you lose for certain; and the greater the number of your tickets the nearer you approach to this certainty.

ADAM SMITH
The Wealth Of Nations
1776

I've seen a game iv cards start among friends, but I niver see friends in a game iv cards.

FINLEY PETER DUNNE
Mr Dooley on Making a Will
1919

Whoever plays deep must necessarily lose his money or his character.

LORD CHESTERFIELD
1773

The whore and gambler by the state
Licensed build that nation's fate.
> WILLIAM BLAKE (1757-1827)
> *Auguries of Innocence*
> (*c.* 1803)

Life is a gamble at terrible odds – if it was a
bet you wouldn't take it.
> TOM STOPPARD
> *Rosencrantz and Guildenstern are Dead*
> 1967

I am sorry I have not learnt to play at cards. It is very useful in life; it generates kindness and consolidates society.

SAMUEL JOHNSON
quoted by James Boswell in *Journal of a Tour To The Hebrides with Samuel Johnson*
1773

You cannot differ with a Californian in the slightest matter without his backing his opinion with a bet.

WILLIAM H. BREWER
US professor
1860

Gambling is fiercer than tigers.

PEOPLE'S DAILY (CHINA'S COMMUNIST PARTY NEWSPAPER)
1944

Glenda Jackson produced the sort of argument which could only come from a Labour MP for Hampstead. Sunday betting was a bad idea because it would encourage oiks to hang around betting shops causing a disturbance. Having a nasty, common McDonalds in the high street is bad enough for all those

well-heeled champions of the proletariat but yobs outside the bookies on a Sunday? Simply ghastly!
ROBERT HARDMAN

He who breaks the bank today, will assuredly return to be broken by the bank tomorrow.
FRANÇOIS BLANC (*b*. 1806)
the founder of the Monte Carlo Casino

There is nothing in the Ten Commandments against gambling. Indeed, it fits in very well with what the Scriptures teach us, for we are told to get rid of our worldly possessions, and gambling is the easiest, quickest and pleasantest way of doing so.
GENERAL PIERRE POLOVTSOFF
Monte Carlo Casino
1937

French law allows a husband to forbid his wife to enter the Casino, and many of them take advantage of this protection.
GENERAL PIERRE POLOVTSOFF
Monte Carlo Casino
1937

God made your balls a little bigger. You're too
good.

CHIP REESE
world-rated poker player on losing $2mil-
lion to 43-year-old upstart gambler
Archie Karas, a Greek who arrived in Las
Vegas with $50 which he turned into
$20million in a year.
Racing Post
13 June 1994

I'm a poker player really, not a dice player. When you play poker you're taking on a human being. They're flesh and blood and they can be scared easily.

But when you play craps you can't scare the dice. They're just plastic.

I'm the biggest gambler in the history of the world. My secret is that I'm fearless. My instincts tell me when to go to the table and when to leave.

All other gamblers win a bit and then stop. I just carry on until I think I've won enough for the time being.

If I lose it is like a kick in the stomach. It makes me feel sick.

ARCHIE KARAS
reported by Nick Szeremeta in the *Racing Post*, 13 June 1994
a fascinating insight into the mind of a big gambler

Gambling, of no matter what kind, is thus a conscious and deliberate departure from the general aim of civilised society, which is to obtain proper value for its money. The gambler, on the other hand, receives either a great deal more than he gives or nothing at all.

RALPH NEVILL
author of *Light Come Light Go*, 1909

One of the most remarkable things about gambling is that no-one ever seems to win – certainly the vast majority of those addicted to play, even the most lucky, generally declare that on the whole they have lost.

RALPH NEVILL
Light Come Light Go
1909

To the gambler fortune appears to be an occult power, the aid of which is not infrequently invoked by means of various fanciful fetishes, which for the moment acquire a real virtue, as being likely to propitiate the invisible influence which presides over speculation.

RALPH NEVILL
Light Come Light Go
1909

Every game of chance presents two kinds of chances which are very distinct – namely, those relating to the person interested (the player) and those inherent in the combinations of the game.

RALPH NEVILL
Light Come Light Go
1909
Ignore this at your peril!

He says that if he won, people would say it was rigged. And if he lost, they'd say he was stupid.

SUSAN JETTON
Speechwriter on behalf of her boss, Louisiana governor, 'Fast' Eddie Edwards, who had announced that he would not be using the casinos which he lobbied hard to bring to the state
The Guardian
3 June 1994

Gambling is going to save this city.

JOHN LINDREY
The Guardian
3 June 1994
Louisiana casino investor on New Orleans

In God I trust, and a fart for the Pope.

THE REPORTED COMMENTS OF A CERTAIN WILLIAM ST LEGER
after he had the good fortune to win a prize of 1s3d (approx 6p) in the Elizabethan National Lottery of 1568. Lottery expert John Bradley of West Midlands, recording the comment, called it 'an illustration of the vigorous anti-Catholic prejudice after the reformation'

The art of the gamble is to bet slightly more than you can afford. Defeat must have its pang or there is no joy in victory.

SIMON BARNES
The Times
1 June 1994

Should I win £1million . . . I will insist on being paid in cash, stuff the money into an industrial strength bin-liner, take a taxi to Heathrow, a plane to Paris, and then a train from the Gare du Nord to the Normandy town of Deauville. The night will be spent in the casino, where, in a spirit of caution no more than £100,000 will be lost on the number 17, its chevals and carriers, and tomorrow morning – having watched the sun rise over the sea and taken a light breakfast – I will take the bin liner to the nearest estate agent, buy a house at the far end of the beach and – sending for my wife and a few possessions – will have completed the move by sundown.

MATTHEW NORMAN
Evening Standard
1 June 1994

It wouldn't have been exciting if it had been for matchsticks
CHRIS BOYD
6 February 1994
Understatement of the year from Chris Boyd who gambled £150,000 life savings on a single spin of the roulette wheel — and won

The National Lottery . . . is a colossal Treasury rip-off and a testament of despair. To take part is to subject oneself to a ruthless exercise in triple taxation.
BRYAN APPLEYARD
Independent
2 November 1994

I call a gambler a person who bets what he can't afford . . . . Getting out of your depth: that's gambling.
WILLIAM HILL (*d*. 1971)
the late founder of the eponymous book-making company

Prostitution may be the oldest profession but I bet there was someone laying odds about whether she would or whether she wouldn't.

RON POLLARD
former Ladbrokes Director

The National Lottery – the ultimate licence to print money; the ultimate computer fraud. Both will happen, you could bet on it.

GUY PARKER OF BRAUNTON, DEVON
letter to *The Times*
28 May 1994

Betting, boozing and buying seem pathetic alternatives to a day set apart for rest and worshipping the Living God.

THE REVD WILLIAM WALLACE
Daily Record
27 May 1994
a member of the Board of Social Responsibility of the Church of England, regretting the advent of Sunday betting and shop opening.
He might well be right but the result of a referendum might just go against his view!

It is completely and utterly wrong for the government to award the lottery and profits to a handful of companies when they are not taking any risks. With this particular business there is no risk – it's a licence to print money.

RICHARD BRANSON
Daily Record
26 May 1994
whose UK Lottery Foundation failed to win the right to run the National Lottery despite his pledge to run it on a non-profit-making basis

The purchase of a lottery ticket is not in itself evil, but it is wrong to stimulate expenditure on gambling through the National Lottery in the knowledge that poor people will be harmed.

> statement from the Methodist Church which 'plans to keep its shares in companies in the lottery consortium Camelot because this would give it a chance to "limit the harm" caused by the lottery'.

The psychology of lottery players is blindingly simple. I love the idea of handing over unspent coppers to my local lottery salesman and waking up on Monday a millionaire.

> MARTIN VANDER WEYER
> *Daily Telegraph*
> 26 May 1994

Imagine the freedom.

> ONTARIO LOTTERY
> 1994
> a stunningly simple yet evocative slogan

The secret of gambling is quitting while you're ahead. And nobody does.
ROBBIE COLTRANE
Sporting Life
29 December 1993
Actor

If you can't spot the sucker in the game in the first ten minutes, then it must be you.
VALUABLE ADVICE TO NOVICE POKER-PLAYERS FROM OLD HANDS.

If the Lord had wanted you to hold on to your money he'd have made it with handles on.
JACK STRAUSS
1982 World Poker Champion

Any innocuous activity can be abused if it is indulged in to excess. But, as a matter of general principle, we don't take the view that – because a very small minority might not be able to control themselves or might abuse the freedoms that we have in society – therefore we should deny those freedoms to everybody else.

I cannot see that as a result of the changes proposed here, which I personally warmly support, that the nation will suddenly be plunged into a hell-hole of gambling the like of which we have never seen before.

> NEIL HAMILTON
> *Sporting Life*
> 11 May 1994
> Junior Trade and Industry Minister, supporting the introduction of Sunday opening of betting shops

This man plays for stakes high enough to induce vertigo yet the eyes are unblinking as the brain behind them gauges the odds, calculates the percentages and waits for his sixth sense to tell him when someone else at the table has made a mistake.

> *Daily Mail*
> 21 April 1994
> pen picture of reigning World Poker Champion, Jim Bechtel

Never tell her how much you win. Never tell her how much you lose. But never lose the house.

JIM BECHTEL
Daily Mail
21 April 1994
recipe for a happy marriage à la Jim Bechtel, World Poker champion 1993

The court declared that despite being recreational in its nature, a lottery is to be regarded as an 'economic activity' and is, therefore, subject to union law. Furthermore, it is an activity which is in the nature of a service, one of the fundamental freedoms of the European Union. Therefore, in principle, the Germans were entitled to offer their lottery to UK citizens.

The real question, though, was whether the UK's obstructive laws were justifiable. Again, in principle, such restrictions are unlawful but the court felt that account had to be taken of the place of gambling in society. Member states over-regulate the practice of gambling to maintain order in society. Questions of public policy are the preserve of national authorities and only they can assess the desirability of restrictions . . . the British ban was upheld.

JOSEPH DALBY
The European
11-18 April 1994
fascinating summary of a European Union case brought to the Court of Justice when German lottery organizers endeavoured to flood the then untapped UK market only to be blocked by UK Customs authorities

When I knocked over the lantern, I was winning.

LOUIS M. COHN
who on his death in 1942 left papers which revealed that an accident with a lantern in a barn in which he was playing the dice game craps in 1871 had started the great fire of Chicago which swept through the entire city.

'No matter how far you travel, or how smart you get,' said the father to the would-be professional gambler son, 'Always remember this: someday a guy is going to come up to you and show you a nice, brand new deck of cards on which the seal is never broken, and this guy is going to offer to bet you that the Jack of Spades will jump out of the deck and squirt cider in your ear. Son, do not bet him, for as sure as you do, you are going to get an ear full of cider.'

DAMON RUNYON

The surest way to beat Las Vegas is to get off the plane that has taken you there and walk straight into the propeller.

ED REID AND OVID DEMARIS
The Truth about Las Vegas
1963
cautionary advice to Las Vegas gamblers

People in the rest of the world merely go broke and die broke. In Vegas, you live broke.

SHERLOCK FELDMAN
Casino pit boss
1963

Gambling interests are like a teenage boy in the back seat of a car with a date. It's always 'I'll go this far and no farther'.

DARRELL HANSON
Racing Post
30 March 1994
Iowa state legislator Darrell Hanson after betting limits on riverboats were removed and slot machines were okayed at race-tracks in the state

Do not trust nor contend
Nor lay wagers, nor lend
And you'll have peace to your life's end.
THOMAS FULLER (1608-61)
Gnomologia

Gambling is a disease of barbarians superficially civilized
DEAN W. R. INGE
Wit and Wisdom of Dean W. R. Inge

Keep flax from fire, youth from gaming.
BENJAMIN FRANKLIN (1706-90)
Poor Richard

Gambling in its varied forms is more widespread than in any previous period of our history
E. BENSON PERKINS
1950
Former Assistant Secretary of the Temperance and Social Welfare Department of the Methodist Church; Chairman of the Churches committee on Gambling; author of *Gambling In English Life*
[surely not a case of 'he would say that'?]

Gambling is more accurately described as a propensity intimately associated with the element of risk, which fascinates and attracts the human species.

E. BENSON PERKINS
1950

Gambling is the stay-at-home, squalid, imaginary, mechanical, anaemic and unlovely adventure of those who have never been able to encounter or create the real, necessary and salutary adventure of life.

MAURICE MAETERLINCK
recorded by E. Benson Perkins, *Gambling in English Life*, 1950
Mr Maeterlinck sounds just the type to take out for an enjoyable evening at the casino.

In truth the foundation of the Lottery is so radically vicious that Your Commitee feel convinced that, under no system of regulations which can be devised, will it be possible for Parliament to adopt it as an efficient source of revenue and at the same time divest it of all the Evils and Calamaties of which it has hitherto proved so baneful a source . . . . Your Committee find, that by the effects of the Lottery, even under its present restrictions, idleness, dissipation, and poverty are increased; the most sacred and confidential trusts are betrayed; domestic comfort is destroyed; madness often created; crimes, subjecting the perpetrators of them to the punishment of death, are common; and even suicide is produced.

PARLIAMENTARY SELECT COMMITTEE, 1808

A Lottery is a Taxation
On all the Fools in Creation
And Heaven be prais'd
It's easily rais'd
Credulity's always in Fashion.
For Folly's a Fund
Will never lose Ground
While Fools are so rife in the Nation.

HENRY FIELDING
song performed at the Drury Lane
Theatre in 1732 in his play *The Lottery*

Unless one gambled freely it was quite impossible to be counted a gentleman, or, for that
matter, a lady of fashion, in the Court of
Charles the Second

CYRIL HUGHES HARTMANN
Games and Gamesters of the Restoration,
1674-1714
1930

Gaming is the very mother of all lies;
And of deceit and cursed villanies,
Manslaughter, blasphemy, and wasteful
sore
Of cattle and time. And furthermore
'Tis shameful and repugnant to honour
To be regarded as a hazarder.

GEOFFREY CHAUCER (*c.* 1343-1400)

If you say you are a Christian when you are a dice player, you say you are what you are not, for you are a partner with the world.

TERTRULLIAN (*c*. AD 150)
Roman writer

Gambling is an agreement between two parties whereby the transfer of something of value, from one to the other, is made dependent upon an uncertain event, in such a way that the gain of one party is balanced by the loss of another.

CANON PETER GREEN
Gambling and Betting, 1924

Gambling consists in taking the risk of winning from or losing to another person without creating anything of human or social value.

MAURICE PARMELEE
American quoted by E. Benson Perkins in
Gambling in English Life, 1950

Gambling is an appeal to chance with two ends in view, the first to give expression to an inherent love of sport or adventure in man,

the second to determine ownership of property. These two ends ultimately come into con-
flict and the second generally destroys the
first.
DR R.H. CHARLES
Gambling and Betting
1924

Gambling is a kind of action by which pleasure is obtained at the cost of pain to another
. . . . Benefit received does not imply effort
put forth, and the happiness of the winner
implies the misery of the loser.
HERBERT SPENCER
Gambling and Betting
1924

The mode of transferring property without
any intermediate good.
DR SAMUEL JOHNSON (1709-84)
Definition of gambling

Over-indulgence in gambling, like excessive
smoking and drinking, can scar the spirit, but
it can never be stopped by legal action. Such
legislation is neither desirable nor effective
because it has never been accepted by the vast

majority of the people. If thrust below ground control falls into the hands of undesirable elements who exploit to the full what to most people is a pleasant and innocuous pastime.

J. PHILIP JONES
Gambling Yesterday and Today
1973

It should not be forgotten that gambling is a multi-million pound business because people enjoy it.

HOME OFFICE REPORT
February 1978

It might be said that gambling is for those perverse people who want nothing for something.

PAUL WEAVER
The Guardian
18 March 1994

The doctor predicted that one day I would leave it in the Coach and Horses if somebody can strike a bet with me which will get me to take it off in the first place.

JEFFREY BERNARD
The Spectator
12 March 1994
on his newly acquired artificial leg.